"Now I'll listen carefully
for your voice and wait
to hear whatever you say..."
Psalm 85:8 (TPT)

Linda Downey

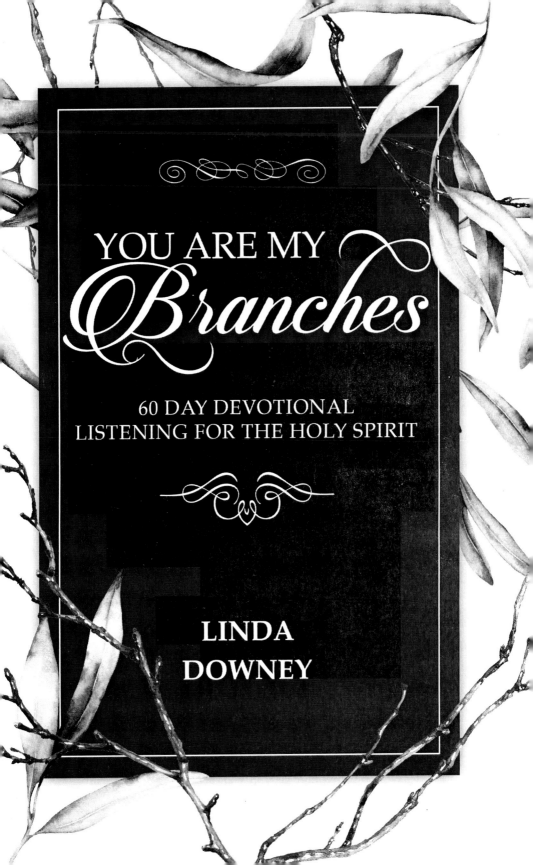

YOU ARE MY
Branches

60 DAY DEVOTIONAL
LISTENING FOR THE HOLY SPIRIT

LINDA
DOWNEY

You Are My Branches

Copyright © 2020 by Linda Downey

Print ISBN: 978-1-09832-568-8

eBook ISBN: 978-1-09832-569-5

Printed in USA

Contents

INTRODUCTION

Pursuing a close and deepening relationship with our Heavenly Father, Jesus and the Holy Spirit, through listening to the voice of the Holy Spirit and meditating on God's written Word, is essential for understanding and following God's specific plan and purpose for our lives. True friendship with the Holy Spirit is God's desire for every believer in Christ. Jesus says in John 14:16-17 (TPT), "And I will ask the Father and he will give you another Savior, the Holy Spirit of Truth, who will be to you a friend just like me—and he will never leave you. The world won't receive him because they can't see him or know him. But you will know him intimately, because he will make his home in you and will live inside of you."

God is eager to speak to us through his Spirit when we are humble and open to hearing the desires of his heart. When I began pursuing a deeper relationship with the Holy Spirit, I humbled myself before the Lord and asked him to forgive me for any pride I had allowed to come into my life that would hold me back from complete surrender of my life to him. I asked the Holy Spirit to come and fill me with more of his presence, as I wanted to better know him as my friend. The following Bible verse immediately came to mind: "I am the sprouting vine and you're my branches. As you live in union with me as your source, fruitfulness will stream from within

you—but when you live separated from me you are powerless."
John 15:5 (TPT)

Perhaps you are desiring a deeper understanding of the Holy Spirit or how to hear the voice of God's Spirit and feel his presence more tangibly every day. If so, I highly recommend you read the book Glory Carriers by Jennifer Eivaz. This is one of the best books ever written about pursuing the presence of God through friendship with the Holy Spirit. Many Christians have misconceptions about the Holy Spirit as a person, and in her book, Jennifer explains how, as Christians, we are privileged to pursue a relationship with the Holy Spirit and have daily conversation with him. God wants to reveal himself to us by the voice of his Spirit and guide us in his purposes for our lives.

During my journey to experience a greater presence of God's Spirit in my life, I often asked the Holy Spirit to help my spiritual ears to hear clearly whatever he wanted to say to me, and to open my spiritual eyes to see what he was doing in the world around me. Soon after, during this daily time of worship, prayer (my conversation with the Lord) and meditating on God's written Word, the Holy Spirit began reaching deep into my heart to gently cleanse and heal me. He revealed past hurts that I had buried, and he helped me to forgive others for things that they had said or done, some of which I had completely forgotten about. This process began an inner healing in me greater than I had ever experienced before. I began to walk in a new level of freedom in my life. I felt peace and joy welling up inside of me, and it fueled my passion to know my Heavenly Father, Jesus and the Holy Spirit even more intimately. In less than a year of pursing a deeper friendship with the Holy Spirit, the transformation that occurred in my life was astounding. I was delivered from 15 years of severe depression, and since then I have not required any medication. I was supernaturally and instantly healed from years of severe abdominal pain due to pancreatic insufficiency, and I also began to see supernatural healing in others when we would agree together in prayer.

John 10:27 (NKJV) says, "My sheep hear my voice, and I know them, and they follow me." It was during my conversational times in prayer that I began using a notebook to journal. When I asked the Holy Spirit to speak to me, I would intentionally listen for him. Soon I would hear the voice of the Holy Spirit speaking to my spirit in a spontaneous flow of thought. I would write down whatever I heard him say. I was surprised by all the good things I would hear. These words were so much sweeter and more encouraging than I would ever think of on my own. I knew that Satan would not speak such beautiful and amazing things about God's kingdom and God's love for me, so I trusted that I must be hearing God's voice through the Holy Spirit. Over time, I began to recognize his voice more clearly, and I could discern when my own thoughts were creeping in.

If you do not know whether or not you are hearing the Lord speaking to you through the Holy Spirit, you should ask yourself some questions: 1) Is what I am hearing contradictory to God's written Word? God never contradicts himself; and 2) Does what I am hearing speak life or death about myself or others? The Holy Spirit will always speak life, and he does so with love, even when our Heavenly Father corrects us. He never condemns or speaks negatively about you or others. Satan uses deception as a major weapon to destroy our lives, and he is eager to use our own thoughts about ourselves and others, caused by our past emotional wounds, to deceive us into thinking our negative thoughts are from the Lord. Even if God chooses to tell you about sin in someone else's life, it is for the purpose of bringing them life through our prayers of intercession for them, not for us to judge or condemn them. God will sometimes speak through his Spirit to warn you about something or someone in order to protect you. He always welcomes further conversation with him, if you need more wisdom or understanding. When God speaks something that changes the direction of your life, it is important to ask him for confirmation in his written Word and for confirmation from other mature believers, especially the spiritual leaders in your life.

I depend on God's written Word as the absolute Truth for how I live my life each day, and how I discern what I am hearing in my thoughts. I have grown to understand from the written Word that our Lord desires to speak to us prophetically through the voice of the Holy Spirit. Jesus says in John 16:13-14 (TPT),

> "But when the truth-giving Spirit comes, he will unveil the reality of every truth within you. He won't speak his own message, but only what he hears from the Father, and he will reveal prophetically to you what is to come. He will glorify me on the earth, for he will receive from me what is mine and reveal it to you."

The personal words spoken through the Holy Spirit to our spirit give us more specific steps for how God wants us to walk in life, such as whom to build relationships with, whom to intercede for in prayer or which job opportunity he has planned for us. As we talk openly and transparently about our lives with the Heavenly Father, Jesus and the Holy Spirit as individual persons, we begin to recognize God's voice and the many ways he speaks and relates to us. He desires a two-way conversation with us, where we share with him our hearts, and then we intentionally take time to listen to what is on his heart.

As we spend time worshipping the Lord, we allow him to heal us, remove the strongholds inside of us from our past experiences, and fill our hearts with new thoughts and dreams for our future. Just one word from him can change our lives forever. All we need is a quiet place to go to every day; a place where we can eliminate the distractions and listen to what he has to say. It does not take long before we are able to hear him speaking in many different ways throughout the day.

If you have never journaled what you feel the Lord is saying to you, I encourage you to do so. I discovered that initially it was easiest to hear him during or right after times of worship, when I would feel the Lord's presence. Just ask the Holy Spirit to speak to you and be ready to write as you listen. Be patient, as there may be only a few words that flow into your thoughts, or you may just see a picture of something in your mind. Write down whatever you feel he might be saying to you and talk with him about it; he will begin to tell you more. Remember, it is important to confirm that what you hear aligns with his written Word, and that it also speaks words of life, and not death, about you or others. If you feel what you hear or see may be a warning, then ask the Lord more about it and begin to intercede in prayer. Finally, it is essential in our walk with the Lord that we are obedient when he asks us to do something. If we are quick to obey what he says, he will be eager to tell us even more. If what he says is changing the direction of your life, then ask him to confirm it with his written Word as well as your spiritual leaders.

It was never my plan to share in a devotional book any of the spoken words I received from the Holy Spirit for my life. Then one day, while I was in prayer, I felt led by the Holy Spirit to share just a few of the words he had spoken to me over the years, as it reflected his heart toward each of us. I have learned through my Christian walk that the way the Holy Spirit chooses to express his words and his presence varies. We are all uniquely created with individual personalities, and no two friendships are exactly the same. However, God's desire is for all of his children to know and experience more of his love and to know his voice as the Holy Spirit speaks.

The few personal conversations I felt led to share in this devotional are those which are very general and encouraging and are not intended for giving direction to anyone but me. My hope is that these daily devotionals will encourage, edify and comfort you as you read them. The amazing result of a friendship with the Holy Spirit is the beautiful and inevitable transformation in one's life. We become more like Jesus, and in turn we are able to be his branch extended to others, bearing much fruit. My prayer for you is that you continually hear the Lord, both through his written Word and the voice of the Holy Spirit, and that you experience and complete all that he has planned for your life.

Day 1

A Year of Blessings and Miracles

If you knew all that this next year holds for you, you would gasp. It is something that your spirit is able to receive but would overwhelm your mind and emotions. This is why you must watch it unfold one day at a time; one miracle, one answered prayer, one blessing at a time. Some blessings and miracles will be very large and become testimonies you will share for a lifetime. Others will show you my goodness and provision for each step in your day. My hand will grab hold of yours because you are my child, and I will teach you how to walk over the rocks and along the river. There will be times when my Spirit will scoop you up and take you deep into my river where the water runs strong and swift and will carry you far. So enjoy our days together this year, and next year when you look back you will shake your head in awe and wonder at all that I have done for you.

Scripture Meditation

Ephesians 1:3 (NIV)

Praise be to the God and Father of our Lord Jesus Christ, who has blessed us in the heavenly realms with every spiritual blessing in Christ.

Hebrews 2:4 (TPT)

Then God added his witness to theirs. He validated their ministry with signs, astonishing wonders, all kinds of powerful miracles, and by *the gifts of* the Holy Spirit, which he distributed as he desired.

Revelation 22:1 (TPT)

Then the angel showed me the river of the water of life, flowing with water clear as crystal, continuously pouring out from the throne of God and of the Lamb.

Day 2

Revelation in God's Word

I am creating something brand new in your life. You already sense in your spirit that change is coming, but you cannot yet see how it will unfold. Your hopes and dreams have repeatedly laid it out for you, and you are doing well to desire my plan for your life. I want you to keep pressing in for the deeper revelation in my written Word. You will discover that my Word not only teaches you how to live successfully and victoriously but it also gives you a powerful tool for revelation in your life. My Word will continue to show you my secrets and how you can attain all that I have waiting for you. Although you understand that my Word does this for you, have you experienced my Word to the point where you depend on it more than your own food every day? Not only does my Word guide you, build your faith and increase your wisdom and knowledge, it gives you the keys to the kingdom that you will need to unlock my mysteries. Seek after my written Word and meditate on it. Look deep and experience a love for my Word like never before.

Scripture Meditation

Deuteronomy 29:29 (NKJV)

"The secret *things belong* to the LORD our God, but those *things which are* revealed *belong* to us and to our children forever, that *we* may do all the words of this law.

Proverbs 2:3-6 (NIV)

...indeed, if you call out for insight and cry aloud for understanding, and if you look for it as for silver and search for it as for hidden treasure, then you will understand the fear of the LORD and find the knowledge of God. For the LORD gives wisdom; from his mouth come knowledge and understanding.

Joshua 1:8 (NKJV)

This Book of the Law shall not depart from your mouth, but you shall meditate in it day and night, that you may observe to do according to all that is written in it. For then you will make your way prosperous, and then you will have good success.

Day 3

Unforgettable Experiences with Him

I always desire to reach into your heart and connect with you on a level we have not experienced before. There will continue to be days in your life that you will never forget. They will stand out like no other. You will be so moved by my insight and revelation, or by your emotional and spiritual experience, that you will write it down so as never to forget what I have done for you. I want you to experience more and more of these days, because my presence and touch in your life changes you forever. One word from me transforms your heart and your life's direction. Will you come to me every day with that kind of anticipation? I want you to come with expectancy that I will do something great for you, and that I have amazing revelation for you in my Word, because I do. I very much want to teach you how to change your life and the world around you. My kingdom come and my will be done on Earth as it is in Heaven! Thank you, my child, for saying, "Yes!" to me today.

Scripture Meditation

Psalm 77:11 (TPT)

Yet I could never forget all your miracles, my God, as I remember all your wonders of old.

Revelation 21:5 (TPT)

And God-Enthroned spoke to me and said, "Consider this! I am making everything to be new and fresh. Write down at once all that I have told you, because each word is trustworthy and dependable."

Matthew 6:10 (AMP)

'Your kingdom come, Your will be done On earth as it is in heaven.'

Day 4

Create in Me a Pure Heart

Do you not see me? Do you not know that it is me revealing your heart and your thoughts? I have the ability to go deep inside of you and cleanse you from all unrighteousness so that you are white as snow, cleansed, holy, perfectly acceptable and pleasing to me. I do this so you can see clearly my will for your life. I am transforming you by renewing your mind, but I am also teaching you to come and humble yourself daily before me so I can repair the broken and missing pieces of your life. I want you to always walk strong and courageously, full of integrity and humility. I will create in you a pure heart whenever you come to me, asking that I do so. Others are there for you as well. You need to lean on the body of Christ. You need them and they need you. I love you my child, and I love that you are teachable and willing to take correction. You will go far, and your destiny will be fulfilled in this lifetime.

Scripture Meditation

Romans 12:2 (NLT)

Don't copy the behavior and customs of this world, but let God transform you into a new person by changing the way you think. Then you will learn to know God's will for you, which is good and pleasing and perfect.

Isaiah 1:18 (NLT)

"Come now, let's settle this," says the Lord. "Though your sins are like scarlet, I will make them as white as snow. Though they are red like crimson, I will make them as white as wool.

Psalm 51:10 (NIV)

Create in me a pure heart, O God, and renew a steadfast spirit within me.

Day 5

Relationship with the Holy Spirit

As you wait before me every day, I just enjoy spending time with you. There is no agenda for our time together today, because I just want you to know how much I love spending time with you. This is what living your life with my Spirit is about; being still in my presence and letting me love on you and surround you with my peace and rest. There are so many wonderful things I have planned for you, and your ability to fulfill your potential grows greater every day as you seek me. Thank you for stretching yourself and learning how to walk in relationship with the Holy Spirit. Isn't he amazing? I love that you reach out to him more each day. Soon you will be in a continual flow with him. Your day-to-day tasks will naturally include him. You will laugh and enjoy every part of your daily walk with him. Then, when the trials come, you will feel him so much closer and his comfort will be like a warm blanket that protects you from the cold. Just let him love you always.

Scripture Meditation

Exodus 33:14 (NIV)

The LORD replied, "My Presence will go with you, and I will give you rest."

Psalm 40:5 (NIV)

Many, LORD my God, are the wonders you have done, the things you planned for us. None can compare with you; were I to speak and tell of your deeds, they would be too many to declare.

2 Corinthians 1:4 (NLT)

He comforts us in all our troubles so that we can comfort others. When they are troubled, we will be able to give them the same comfort God has given us.

Day 6

Hearing the Holy Spirit More Clearly

Do you see how I am working with you in different ways than I have before? I am broadening your paradigm, and I need you to hear me clearly. Then you will be able to recognize which doors I am opening, and which doors are simply distractions. Your heart desires more of me, and you are thinking more about the vision for your life and your dreams. That is wonderful, and that is how you will continue to move forward, but I also need you to keep focused on me. Keep listening for me so I can give you more of my plan for your life. You still have many dreams to come and I still have many steps for you to take to prepare you for where we are going. If you can hear me clearly in the Spirit, I will tell you and show you what I am doing. Rest in me. Yes, find my sweet and perfect rest. You will find yourself changed—transformed into a new creation, and my creations are perfect and beautiful in my sight.

Scripture Meditation

Revelation 3:8 (NIV)

I know your deeds. See, I have placed before you an open door that no one can shut. I know that you have little strength, yet you have kept my word and have not denied my name.

Matthew 11:28-30 (NIV)

"Come to me, all you who are weary and burdened, and I will give you rest. Take my yoke upon you and learn from me, for I am gentle and humble in heart, and you will find rest for your souls. For my yoke is easy and my burden is light."

2 Corinthians 5:17 (NLT)

This means that anyone who belongs to Christ has become a new person. The old life is gone; a new life has begun!

Day 7

Eyes that See and Ears that Hear

Each day is special, and I have amazing things planned for you. Wait in my presence and watch. You will begin to see what I am doing. I am also going to tell you what I am doing. Your "eyes that see" are as important as your "ears that hear". Do not develop one without the other. Keep meditating on that concept. My revelation will come. When you make the effort to see and hear me, it is an invitation from you to me, inviting me to do something powerful through you. I never stop watching to see that my word is fulfilled. Rest in my presence. Bask in my love. Fill your heart full of my wisdom, and I will guide you and prepare you for your life's call. You are in training right now, but one day you will teach others how to bring my Kingdom message to those who are lost, poor and hurting. As you bring the broken-hearted to me, I will bind up their wounds and fill them with my love. There is no greater joy they will ever experience than being filled with my love. Thank you for coming alongside me and doing what I have called you to do.

Scripture Meditation

Matthew 13:16 (NLT)

But blessed are your eyes, because they see; and your ears, because they hear.

Jeremiah 1:12 (NIV)

The Lord said to me, "You have seen correctly, for I am watching to see that my word is fulfilled."

Isaiah 61:1 (TPT)

The mighty Spirit of Lord Yahweh is wrapped around me because Yahweh has anointed me, as a messenger to preach good news to the poor. He sent me to heal the wounds of the brokenhearted, to tell captives, "You are free," and to tell prisoners, "Be free from your darkness."

Day 8

When I Walk Through the Valley

Have you ever wondered why I allow you to walk through such difficult times in life? You understand that it makes you stronger and that it helps you depend on me, but did you realize that my greatest strength and my greatest miracles are unveiled when my people are desperate for me? This is true. It is during people's darkest hours that I shine brightest. You can rest assured that I wait for you to come to me as you recognize that I am the only way through your valleys, even the valley of the shadow of death. If you will come to me, you will no longer be afraid. You will discover, in the midst of it all, that my grace is sufficient. You will also discover that my love is much more immense than the struggle that surrounds you. Always look to me. Cry out to me. Let me hear your heart surrender, and I will demonstrate my faithfulness and unchanging love for you. This is when you will be free to receive my miracle, my love and my grace. I love you so much and your pain and struggle cannot separate you from me.

Scripture Meditation

2 Corinthians 12:9 (NLT)

Each time he said, "My grace is all you need. My power works best in weakness." So now I am glad to boast about my weaknesses, so that the power of Christ can work through me.

Psalm 34:17 (NLT)

The LORD hears his people when they call to him for help. He rescues them from all their troubles.

Psalm 139:7-10 (NIV)

Where can I go from your Spirit? Where can I flee from your presence? If I go up to the heavens, you are there; if I make my bed in the depths, you are there. If I rise on the wings of the dawn, if I settle on the far side of the sea, even there your hand will guide me, your right hand will hold me fast.

Day 9

Healing Past Wounds

The refreshing wind of my Spirit that flows through you and around you today is designed to not only fill you with my love, but also to heal some areas in your heart where you still have open wounds from past hurts and offense. Many of these wounds are hidden deep, but I desire to come and reveal to you those areas you have been afraid to go. I will be with you, and where I am there is no need to be afraid. I bring healing and refreshing as we work through these areas together. Let me take you there. Let me show you that I am more than able to heal your heart and fill you with even more of my love and peace. Once these old wounds are healed, they will no longer drain away the love I have placed inside of you. You will be able to sustain that feeling of peace and joy in your life once again. You are my pride and joy and I will fill you with my goodness and strength. Our time together is so precious and powerful, and today you are allowing me to do again what I do best—love you.

Scripture Meditation

Jeremiah 30:17 (NLT)

"I will give you back your health and heal your wounds," says the LORD…

Isaiah 41:10 (NLT)

Don't be afraid, for I am with you. Don't be discouraged, for I am your God. I will strengthen you and help you. I will hold you up with my victorious right hand.

John 14:27 (AMP)

Peace I leave with you; My [perfect] peace I give to you; not as the world gives do I give to you. Do not let your heart be troubled, nor let it be afraid. [Let My perfect peace calm you in every circumstance and give you courage and strength for every challenge.]

Day 10

There Is No One Like Me

If you are willing to take this time to listen to me, then I am ready to tell you something wonderful and remind you of the amazing things I am doing. Take time to close your eyes and listen to what I am saying about you. Do you see what a great person you are in my Kingdom, and how very proud I am of your heart for me? Do not look at others and compare yourself to them. Each one has gifts given to them by me and there is no one else like them. More importantly, though, there is no one like you. I long to see you in the mornings and I love to walk beside you throughout the day. When you are busy or distracted, you lose awareness of my presence and, at times, believe you are on your own to get things done. Rest assured, I am right here to encourage you, support you and give you wisdom for your daily responsibilities. So take a deep breath and fill yourself with my Spirit, who gives you perfect peace and love. Fill your heart full and know that I am right here taking care of all the details. Enjoy the great plan I have for you, one day at a time, as you reach the people around you.

Scripture Meditation

Psalm 126:2-3 (NLT)

We were filled with laughter, and we sang for joy. And the other nations said, "What amazing things the LORD has done for them." Yes, the LORD has done amazing things for us! What joy!

Romans 12:3-6 (MSG)

I'm speaking to you out of deep gratitude for all that God has given me, and especially as I have responsibilities in relation to you. Living then, as every one of you does, in pure grace, it's important that you not misinterpret yourselves as people who are bringing this goodness to God. No, God brings it all to you. The only accurate way to understand ourselves is by what God is and by what he does for us, not by what we are and what we do for him. In this way we are like the various parts of a human body. Each part gets its meaning from the body as a whole, not the other way around. The body we're talking about is Christ's body of chosen people. Each of us finds our meaning and function as a part of his body. But as a chopped-off finger or cut-off toe we wouldn't amount to much, would we? So since we find ourselves fashioned into all these excellently formed and marvelously functioning parts in Christ's body, let's just go ahead and be what we were made to be, without enviously or pridefully comparing ourselves with each other, or trying to be something we aren't.

Day 11

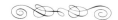

Navigating God's Plan

As the day rolls on and the night comes, I put in order all those things that you have labored to accomplish throughout the day. I start something fresh and new as you sleep. I put all the plans I have for you in motion and I watch you throughout the new day as you navigate my plan. Sometimes it feels like a gauntlet and sometimes like a maze, but I will always make clear the beautiful pathway to my heart and my kingdom in front of you. Come into my presence. Come into my banqueting table and receive all the revelation and wisdom you desire. It is more than you could ever taste of, and it is all so amazingly prepared. So do not worry about the obstacles or the mysteries, just feast and you will see the answers clearly from my perspective looking down. The answers are right there, just outside the gauntlet and the maze. You will see these answers from up here with me. This is always the best place to find them. Come close with me and see what I see. This is what brings me such pleasure and joy—sitting beside you, watching you discover my hidden treasures that are just for you.

Scripture Meditation

Psalm 8:3-6 (NLT)

When I look at the night sky and see the work of your fingers—the moon and the stars you set in place—what are mere mortals that you should think about them, human beings that you should care for them? Yet you made them only a little lower than God and crowned them with glory and honor. You gave them charge of everything you made, putting all things under their authority—

2 Corinthians 4:16-18 (TPT)

So no wonder we don't give up. For even though our outer person gradually wears out, our inner being is renewed every single day. We view our slight, short-lived troubles in the light of eternity. We see our difficulties as the substance that produces for us an eternal, weighty glory far beyond all comparison, because we don't focus our attention on what is seen but on what is unseen. For what is seen is temporary, but the unseen realm is eternal.

Day 12

The Whisper of His Voice

There are times when you stop to listen for me, and you wonder what I would like to share with you. The beauty in this act of listening is that I will always speak something fresh and encouraging. This helps you look forward to hearing from me and take note of what I have to say. It is important to quiet yourself so you can hear my whisper. It does not have to be physically quiet around you, but your spirit and your thoughts need to be quieted in order to hear me accurately. I want you to associate my presence in our alone time with gentleness, kindness and love, because I love you much more than you are able to comprehend. I continually show you more of my love as you enlarge your capacity to receive it. Push wide open the door to your heart, and let me lavish my love upon you more abundantly each day.

Scripture Meditation

Proverbs 8:34 (TPT)

If you wait at wisdom's doorway, longing to hear a word for every day, joy will break forth within you as you listen for what I'll say.

Psalm 131:2 (NLT)

Instead, I have calmed and quieted myself, like a weaned child who no longer cries for its mother's milk. Yes, like a weaned child is my soul within me.

Ephesians 3:18-19 (TPT)

Then you will be empowered to discover what every holy one experiences—the great magnitude of the astonishing love of Christ in all its dimensions. How deeply intimate and far-reaching is his love! How enduring and inclusive it is! Endless love beyond measurement that transcends our understanding—this extravagant love pours into you until you are filled to overflowing with the fullness of God!

Day 13

His Presence in Every Moment

Do you understand that no matter your circumstances, no matter your timeline for getting where you are going, I am in the midst of it all? I am outside of time. I Am Who I Am. I look for you in every part of your life, and in every aspect of your day. Just stop, look, listen and feel my heartbeat. I am your source of strength and wisdom for each decision and each moment of weakness. You can just breathe me in and sense my fullness come in and meet your need. Do not worry about not having enough time with me. I am glad you want to put me first every day, and I am glad you want to grow in strength and in your authority over your body, soul and spirit. It is equally important to me, however, that you sense my presence every moment of the day so that you feel continually refreshed and loved. I want to guide you in the right things to say and do in order to bring forth my best plan for your life and the lives of others. You are so loved, and it is my heart's desire to give you my very best. Are you ready to receive it?

Scripture Meditation

Psalm 90:2 (NIV)

Before the mountains were born or you brought forth the whole world, from everlasting to everlasting you are God.

Exodus 3:14 (AMP)

God said to Moses, "I Am Who I Am"; and He said, "You shall say this to the Israelites, 'I Am has sent me to you.' "

Psalm 147:5 (AMP)

Great is our [majestic and mighty] Lord and abundant in strength; His understanding is inexhaustible [infinite, boundless].

Day 14

Peace Rather Than Worry

When you think about the day or week ahead, I do not want you to worry about how to get everything done because I will make things plain and clear for you. I want you to look at each day like a blank chalkboard, just waiting for me to teach you what you need to learn. I will give you the keys to every situation you will face. I want you to have complete confidence in me to bring all the elements together at just the right time. It is walking in this dependency on me that will bring you such amazing peace. You do not have to worry about the details because they will come to you as you need them. Enjoy this day of not worrying about getting things done. Remember that worrying is just a mindset. You have all the time in the world to enjoy each day to the fullest with no regrets. I love you, and I will take care of your every need. I hear your every request, and I am happy to fulfill them when it draws you closer to my plans for your life.

Scripture Meditation

Psalm 32:8 (NLT)

The LORD says, "I will guide you along the best pathway for your life. I will advise you and watch over you."

Matthew 6:33-34 (NIV)

But seek first his kingdom and his righteousness, and all these things will be given to you as well. Therefore do not worry about tomorrow, for tomorrow will worry about itself. Each day has enough trouble of its own.

Psalm 16:11 (AMP)

You will show me the path of life; In Your presence is fullness of joy; In Your right hand there are pleasures forevermore.

Day 15

God Loves My Voice

I eagerly wait to hear you speak to me, just as you desire to hear my voice. Even though I know your thoughts and your next move, I still love to hear your voice as you talk to me and intimately share with me what's on your heart. Your voice is what brings us into dialogue, which in turn brings you into a closer relationship with me. Your voice is the way I communicate with others as well, and my love for them is often shared through your voice. You may or may not realize it, but I am using your voice every day. So think about what you are saying to others, and reflect on when and how I am using your spoken words. Your voice is powerful, and when it is combined with my thoughts and my words, there is nothing you cannot accomplish. Let your voice be heard, and let the nations rejoice!

Scripture Meditation

2 Chronicles 7:15-16 (NIV)

Now my eyes will be open and my ears attentive to the prayers offered in this place. I have chosen and consecrated this temple so that my Name may be there forever. My eyes and my heart will always be there.

Proverbs 16:24 (TPT)

Then you will be empowered to discover what every holy one experiences—the great magnitude of the astonishing love of Christ in all its dimensions. How deeply intimate and far-reaching is his love! How enduring and inclusive it is! Endless love beyond measurement that transcends our understanding—this extravagant love pours into you until you are filled to overflowing with the fullness of God!

Psalm 96:2-3 (TPT)

Don't stop! Keep on singing! Make his name famous! Tell everyone every day how wonderful he is. Give them the good news of our great Savior. Take the message of his glory and miracles to every nation. Tell them about all the amazing things he has done.

Day 16

God's Hidden Treasure

When the night seems long or the road seems narrow, just lay your head upon me. I will comfort you and give you rest. I am here to feed you, quench your thirst and strengthen you on your journey. I am also here to share with you my promises for your future, as well as the treasures that await you. You will need me to help you search them out, however, because without my prompting you to look at certain things differently, you will completely miss these hidden treasures and the many promises I have given you in my Word. Keep in mind that if you focus too much on just my promises for your future, you will miss the hidden treasures along the way. So, continue to enjoy this daily journey with me as much as you look forward to the fulfillment of future promises. When you feel anxious or overwhelmed, just remember I am right here with you and you may rest your head upon me. Let me give you some food and refresh you, because I am excited to continue on this treasure hunt with you.

Scripture Meditation

Psalm 116:7 (TPT)

Now I can say to myself and to all, "Relax and rest, be confident and serene, for the Lord rewards fully those who simply trust in him."

Isaiah 45:3 (NIV)

I will give you hidden treasures, riches stored in secret places, so that you may know that I am the LORD, the God of Israel, who summons you by name.

Psalm 119:76 (NIV)

May your unfailing love be my comfort, according to your promise to your servant.

Day 17

Am I Hindering God's Presence?

There are days you when you wonder if you are hindering my presence or stifling the flow of the Holy Spirit. But I tell you the truth, there is no mountain too big, no valley too low and no emotion too deep to separate you from the love I have for you. I am here with you in the midst of every circumstance. You never hinder me when you seek my face. At times your spiritual ears and eyes are shut, and you cannot hear me or see what I am doing around you as clearly as you would like. Nevertheless, I have my arms wrapped around you holding you close with your head in my neck and my kisses on your face. Softly I speak to you and bring you into a place of rest with me. I know that your heart and mind will heal in my presence, and your spirit will be filled fresh with my Spirit. The body of Christ will also help me to build you up into that confident, joyful person you were created to be, ready to take on the world with victory! No obstacle is too great, and no sorrow too much to bear, because my love prevails over death and darkness. My love rules the universe, and I am here for you today. I love you just the same as I always have and always will.

Scripture Meditation

Romans 8:38-39 (TPT)

So now I live with the confidence that there is nothing in the universe with the power to separate us from God's love. I'm convinced that his love will triumph over death, life's troubles, fallen angels, or dark rulers in the heavens. There is nothing in our present or future circumstances that can weaken his love. There is no power above us or beneath us—no power that could ever be found in the universe that can distance us from God's passionate love, which is lavished upon us through our Lord Jesus, the Anointed One!

Hebrews 10:23-25 (TPT)

So now we must cling tightly to the hope that lives within us, knowing that God always keeps his promises! Discover creative ways to encourage others and to motivate them toward acts of compassion, doing beautiful works as expressions of love. This is not the time to pull away and neglect meeting together, as some have formed the habit of doing, because we need each other! In fact, we should come together even more frequently, eager to encourage and urge each other onward as we anticipate that day dawning.

Day 18

Deeper and Deeper in His Presence

Each day when you come into my presence it may seem as though I become better than ever before, but my love for you, my goodness and my faithfulness never change. You are just experiencing what it feels like to go deeper and deeper into this love, and my love is limitless. You can go as deep as you are able to go, and you will only dip beneath the surface of what I can give you. You do not need to strive hard to reach me. Instead, just sit and wait for me to come over you, wave after wave. Soon you will begin to transform, and you will see what I have coming to you. All you have to do is wait for me. My Word and my promises will come as sure as the waves come toward the seashore. My goodness and my plans for you are coming. Just close your eyes and wait. Suddenly your spiritual eyes will awaken, and you will see my living water running over you. You will then be able to touch anyone around you and see this water spread to them as well. The people that you touch will be changed; transformed by my love.

Scripture Meditation

Psalm 100:4-5 (NIV)

Enter his gates with thanksgiving and his courts with praise; give thanks to him and praise his name. For the Lord is good and his love endures forever; his faithfulness continues through all generations.

Psalm 42:7 (NIV)

Deep calls to deep in the roar of your waterfalls; all your waves and breakers have swept over me.

1 John 4:19 (TPT)

Our love for others is *our grateful response* to the love God first demonstrated to us.

Day 19

Experiencing Intimacy with The Lord

Here we are in this place, enjoying some time together again. I rejoice that you desire to share my love with others, but our time alone together is more about you and me than it is about others. Serving others comes out of the overflow that is created from time spent with me. Our time together is about the intimacy we are building with one another. It is about us just spending time together talking and sharing. I want to hear about your hopes and dreams, and I want to heal you. Let me set you free from fear and from anything that is holding you back from experiencing all that I intend you to have in your life. We are exploring new things in the Spirit. This is a time of comfort and refreshing. Our time together is like having a nice refreshing drink at a beautiful place on a gorgeous day. It is like walking together with the breezes blowing and the temperature remaining absolutely perfect. This is what our time together is all about. It is the pure pleasure of spending quality time together. Everything else will come out of this intimacy we share. So, let's take this time now and see how enjoyable and helpful my Word will be for you.

Scripture Meditation

Psalm 23:1-4 (TPT)

The Lord is my best friend and my shepherd. I always have more than enough. He offers a resting place for me in his luxurious love. His tracks take me to an oasis of peace, the quiet brook of bliss. That's where he restores and revives my life. He opens before me pathways to God's pleasure and leads me along in his footsteps of righteousness so that I can bring honor to his name. Lord, even when your path takes me through the valley of deepest darkness, fear will never conquer me, for you already have! You remain close to me and lead me through it all the way.

Isaiah 55:2-3 (NLT)

Why spend your money on food that does not give you strength? Why pay for food that does you no good? Listen to me, and you will eat what is good. You will enjoy the finest food. Come to me with your ears wide open. Listen, and you will find life. I will make an everlasting covenant with you. I will give you all the unfailing love I promised to David.

Day 20

Stepping Out in Faith

I love sharing my heart with you because I know you will take the time to listen. I am eager to teach you something new every day, but I am also eager to talk to you about how things are going for you and how you are feeling about this process I am walking you through. I know you have questions, so just keep asking me for the answers. As you read my Word and listen with your spiritual ears to what I am saying, you will begin to recognize that I am giving you the direction you have been seeking. Some steps require that you not question why I am doing things the way that I am, but that you just step out in faith and do what you hear me asking you to do. Do not worry about not hearing me correctly, just step out in faith and I will honor that faith and bring you into new joy and victory in your life. It is your heart of obedience that puts your faith into action. You will be amazed by what doors I open up for you, and the miracles I will perform. I love you and I always have the best plan for your life.

Scripture Meditation

Jeremiah 33:3 (NKJV)

'Call to Me, and I will answer you, and show you great and mighty things, which you do not know.'

2 Corinthians 5:7 (NKJV)

For we walk by faith, not by sight.

1 John 3:22 (NLT)

And we will receive from him whatever we ask because we obey him and do the things that please him.

Day 21

Finding God's Solution to My Problem

Whatever your struggle, it will fade away when you focus your thoughts and affections on me. I desire your heart not only for my own pleasure and purpose, but for your benefit as well. If I can draw your attention to me, I can take care of all your anxious thoughts. I will help you see the solution standing right in front of you. I want you to open your eyes to see clearly the bigger picture surrounding your perceived problem or the enemy's obstacles. Each day I have a life of joy and victory prepared for you, but I need you to stop and focus on me so I can fill you with my Spirit—fresh and new. Then you will see the day ahead with your spiritual eyes rather than your natural eyes. I love you and it is my desire each day to help you acquire everything you need to live victoriously.

Scripture Meditation

Job 11:16 (NIV)

You will surely forget your trouble, recalling it only as waters gone by.

Matthew 5:8 (MSG)

"You're blessed when you get your inside world—your mind and heart—put right. Then you can see God in the outside world."

Psalm 118:15 (NLT)

Songs of joy and victory are sung in the camp of the godly. The strong right arm of the LORD has done glorious things!

Day 22

Battling the Distractions

When you sit down with me and tune out the distractions, we can have a serious heart to heart talk. I know you desire to see my will done on the earth, as well as for me to use you as a part of that plan. You are trying hard to yield to me, but you are still battling the distractions of life. I want you to close your eyes and take a deep breath. Now just listen for a moment. As you focus on what I am showing you and the beauty that I am creating all around you, and particularly right in front of you, it will overtake and push away the distractions. Eventually all you will see is the beauty I have created for you to walk in every single day. This is my peace and prosperity for you. It is a place where the fruit is so numerous and in such a variety that it will be difficult to decide what to enjoy first. I will give you all the time you need each day to taste of my freedom and to walk here beside me so that if you choose, you will be filled with all that you need. When you are satisfied, then you can share it with others.

Scripture Meditation

Philippians 4:8 (TPT)

So keep your thoughts continually fixed on all that is authentic and real, honorable and admirable, beautiful and respectful, pure and holy, merciful and kind. And fasten your thoughts on every glorious work of God, praising him always.

1 Timothy 4:4 (NLT)

Since everything God created is good, we should not reject any of it but receive it with thanks.

Philemon 6 (AMP)

I pray that the sharing of your faith may become effective *and* powerful because of your *accurate* knowledge of every good thing which is ours in Christ.

Day 23

Stepping-Stones to Greatness

Do not let cares and worries come in and take away these precious wonderful moments we have together right now. Did I not take care of you the last time you asked me to take away your fear? So now it is time to just breathe me in again. Take a minute to listen to what I am saying to you. There will never be a day or night or even one single minute when I am not right here with you, teaching you and helping you navigate this beautiful plan I have for you. It is a process you know well, and I enjoy watching how you use your individuality to discover the best way to carry out my plan. I give you many choices and you are using them as stepping-stones to greatness. Your story is unique, and it is a story that will save others from a life of hopelessness. You are leading the way for others to find me, and to discover for themselves that I have been right here helping them and teaching them too. Enjoy this plan I have for you, because it is going to help many more people than you realize. I love you.

Scripture Meditation

1 Peter 5:7 (NLT)

Give all your worries and cares to God, for he cares about you.

Exodus 13:21 (NIV)

By day the LORD went ahead of them in a pillar of cloud to guide them on their way and by night in a pillar of fire to give them light, so that they could travel by day or night.

Hebrews 6:10 (NIV)

God is not unjust; he will not forget your work and the love you have shown him as you have helped his people and continue to help them.

Day 24

The Lord Sees My Beauty

When you look to the heavens to see my throne, to gaze upon my face and to feel my presence in your life, I see beauty far greater than many fields of radiant flowers. You are more beautiful to me than all the birds as they sing and more precious than one drop of dew on the grass. My love has reached your heart and you are now this perfect flower opening into full bloom. Your fragrance fills my nostrils and I am absolutely enveloped in your beauty. It is hard for you to find this kind of beauty at times, especially when the storms of life surround you. But when you show up to meet me, the storm clouds leave and the sun breaks through shining brightly upon you. Your life unfolds before me and gives off the most beautiful fragrance. So thank you, My Love, for coming to meet with me today and for opening your heart to let me shine upon you. You will be fragrant to everyone around you. Let them enjoy all that you are.

Scripture Meditation

Deuteronomy 32:2 (NLT)

Let my teaching fall on you like rain; let my speech settle like dew. Let my words fall like rain on tender grass, like gentle showers on young plants.

Proverbs 10:25 (NLT)

When the storms of life come, the wicked are whirled away, but the godly have a lasting foundation.

Numbers 6:25-26 (NKJV)

The LORD make His face shine upon you, And be gracious to you; The LORD lift up His countenance upon you, And give you peace.

Day 25

Completing the Good Work in Me

As we walk this journey of life together, you will further understand my plans to protect you and secure your spiritual foundations. I come alongside you to shore up your areas of weakness, to help you care for this beautiful temple of yours and to prepare you to continue my purpose for your life. I specialize in carpentry, and I know which areas of your heart and mind need more attention right now, and in which order I need to complete my good work. If you will listen to my instruction, I will teach you the skills and the knowledge you need in order to move forward. Then, not only will you be able to carry out your best work for me, but you can teach others how to do the same. I am ready and willing to teach anyone who is eager to learn and who will, in turn, help others. It should be no surprise to you that I smile while I watch my work completed in you.

Scripture Meditation

Psalm 121:8 (TPT)

You will be guarded by God himself. You will be safe when you leave your home and safely you will return. He will protect you now, and he'll protect you forevermore!

Philippians 4:9 (NLT)

Keep putting into practice all you learned and received from me— everything you heard from me and saw me doing. Then the God of peace will be with you.

Philippians 1:6 (NLT)

And I am certain that God, who began the good work within you, will continue his work until it is finally finished on the day when Christ Jesus returns.

Day 26

What Is God Highlighting Right Now?

All the things surrounding you have some meaning to your life, and they are all important in one aspect or another. The things I specifically highlight for you have to do with something special I am working out in your life. I want you to consider what I am doing and seek me for answers about what you should be doing to help me. There are other areas of your life I am highlighting for the purpose of learning more about me, so you are able to discover some of the mysteries I have not yet revealed to you. I always have new things to teach you and new things to show you, but first I need you to open your spiritual eyes to see what I see. Also, when you come to me with your requests, come eagerly as a child does when they are receiving a gift from a loved one. I am saying to you now, "Begin to unwrap my gift for you." You will see your dreams become reality, and you will experience my love in an even greater measure than before. My heart will rejoice with you because you will be filled with my love and joy!

Scripture Meditation

1 Corinthians 7:17 (TPT)

May all believers continue to live the wonderful lives God has called them to live, according to what he assigns for each person, for this is what I teach to believers everywhere.

Psalm 119:130 (TPT)

Break open your word within me until revelation-light shines out! Those with open hearts are given insight into your plans.

James 1:17 (NLT)

Whatever is good and perfect is a gift coming down to us from God our Father, who created all the lights in the heavens. He never changes or casts a shifting shadow.

Day 27

Dreams Coming Back to Life

Your growth is amazing to watch, and it is largely because you have let my Spirit water and soften your heart. You are willing to let me into those deep places and reveal to you the areas that need my love and healing. Because you have freely given me your heart, I will bring back to life the dreams which have died within you. Some of your dreams have been laid down or forgotten as time has passed, but they are still there waiting for you and I am bringing them back to your attention again. I will show you that this journey with me is the most life-giving experience you will ever know. Do you realize that each time you let my Spirit water your heart, that I am free to pull out the weeds and dig up the treasure you have buried inside of you? Just think about all that we have yet to discover together. Do not stop coming into my presence. I am here, waiting to show you what we are going to accomplish together during your life here on Earth. You are going to see many of your dreams fulfilled!

Scripture Meditation

Jeremiah 24:7 (NLT)

I will give them hearts that recognize me as the LORD. They will be my people, and I will be their God, for they will return to me wholeheartedly.

Isaiah 44:3 (NLT)

For I will pour out water to quench your thirst and to irrigate your parched fields. And I will pour out my Spirit on your descendants, and my blessing on your children.

Isaiah 30:18 (NKJV)

Therefore the LORD will wait, that He may be gracious to you; And therefore He will be exalted, that He may have mercy on you. For the LORD *is* a God of justice; Blessed *are* all those who wait for Him.

Day 28

Just Come into His Presence

When you sleep, I watch over you. When you rise, I set everything in motion to welcome you into my presence. Each time you come to me at the start of the day, I already know what you are thinking and what you are feeling. Your struggles, your hopes and your desires are all known to me. You do not have to struggle to articulate to me what you are going through. Just come. Come into my presence—just you and me—apart from the distractions and the busyness. My angels come as you need them and help usher in the glory that surrounds me as well. I will take care of the urgent needs that you have lined up in your mind. I will give you rest, peace and strength as I provide for you and take care of each one of your needs. But first, you must come to me and let me help you. Let me fill you fresh each morning with my love and joy. It will carry you through all that each day brings. I love you.

Scripture Meditation

Psalm 3:5 (TPT)

So now I'll lie down and sleep like a baby—then I'll awake in safety, for you surround me with your glory.

Psalm 139:2 (TPT)

You perceive every movement of my heart and soul, and you understand my every thought before it even enters my mind.

Psalm 16:11 (NLT)

You will show me the way of life, granting me the joy of your presence and the pleasures of living with you forever.

Day 29

Free from the Strongholds

I see you going after those things I am revealing to you, including areas of your life where you have let pride, insecurity or compromise slip in. Thank you for allowing me to prepare you for the exciting and challenging road that lies ahead. It is beautiful when you let me help you by setting you free from the strongholds that keep you from reaching your destiny. It is a process, but through this process I have many amazing things to teach you. I am going to set you free from strongholds the enemy placed in your life years ago when you were an innocent child and ignorant of things in the spirit. Now that you have matured in your walk with me, these areas need to be uprooted for you to continue to grow and fulfill your destiny. The plan I have for you is much larger than you even imagine, and it can only be realized if you come to me and lay down your pride and ask forgiveness for the areas where you have been compromising. In turn, I will help you forgive others in your past and teach you how to avoid holding on to offense by what others say or do to you in the future. Will you come to me with your whole heart? Let me set you free, heal you and catapult you into your destiny!

Scripture Meditation

Proverbs 29:23 (NKJV)

A man's pride will bring him low, But the humble in spirit will retain honor.

2 Corinthians 10:3-4 (NLT)

We are human, but we don't wage war as humans do. We use God's mighty weapons, not worldly weapons, to knock down the strongholds of human reasoning and to destroy false arguments.

Mark 11:25 (TPT)

And whenever you stand praying, if you find that you carry something in your heart against another person, release him and forgive him so that your Father in heaven will also release you and forgive you of your faults.

Day 30

Frustration and Intimacy

Sometimes you feel a little uncertain during our time together, like you have not received all that you expect or desire to receive. Sometimes you feel frustration that you sleep longer than you should instead of getting up and spending more time with me. Life is about choices and discipline, but you will still walk victoriously as long as we get some uninterrupted time together each day. You need to let your frustration, about not receiving what you were hoping for, spur you to dig deeper and press into my presence throughout the day until you find the peace, wisdom and revelation you are longing for. This creates an even greater level of intimacy between us. I will fill you with more of my Spirit all day long, as you ask me, and refresh you while you sleep. I am touched by every minute spent with you, and I rejoice over the friendship we share.

Scripture Meditation

Matthew 6:6 (TPT)

But whenever you pray, go into your innermost chamber and be alone with Father God, praying to him in secret. And your Father, who sees all you do, will reward you openly.

Psalm 40:16 (NLT)

But may all who search for you be filled with joy and gladness in you. May those who love your salvation repeatedly shout, "The LORD is great!"

Psalm 42:8 (NLT)

But each day the LORD pours his unfailing love upon me, and through each night I sing his songs, praying to God who gives me life.

Day 31

Here I Am Lord

I love watching you. You continue to grow in wisdom and understanding as you discover my plan for your life. I love your eagerness to figure out what I have waiting for you, and your willingness to be obedient when I show you how to proceed. I know that your heart's desire is to never misstep my perfect plan for you. All I need is your heart and your desire to walk out my plan. I will help you with the rest. Just keep coming to me and saying, "Here I am, Lord, send me." I use every part of your day to piece together this magnificent plan. There are truths and mysteries that I desire to reveal to you each day, so it is important that you do not weary of your daily routine. Instead, just keep coming to me so that I can open your eyes and help you understand what I am doing with you. Enjoy our time together each day and rejoice over each new piece I reveal to you. I love you my precious child.

Scripture Meditation

Psalm 32:8 (NIV)

I will instruct you and teach you in the way you should go; I will counsel you with my loving eye on you.

Isaiah 6:8 (NIV)

Then I heard the voice of the Lord saying, "Whom shall I send? And who will go for us?" And I said, "Here am I. Send me!"

Galatians 6:9 (TPT)

And don't allow yourselves to be weary or disheartened in planting good seeds, for the season of reaping the wonderful harvest you've planted is coming!

Day 32

No More Fear

You are beginning to see what I have longed for you to see—that I have made a way for you where there is no fear. There is no path too narrow or too dangerous to walk. There is no obstacle too big to overcome. The mountains will crash into the sea with one word from me. I will take you places you never thought possible, because you will receive the revelation of my unwavering protection around you. It is imperative that you do not focus on the trouble surrounding you, otherwise you will take your eyes off me and where we are going. As your love for me grows, and your passion to follow me anywhere dominates your thoughts, you will easily bypass all the traps and obstacles the enemy tries to put in front of you. Just keep looking forward in the Spirit to see where all of the answers await you. Have a beautiful day, My Love.

Scripture Meditation

1 John 4:18 (NLT)

Such love has no fear, because perfect love expels all fear. If we are afraid, it is for fear of punishment, and this shows that we have not fully experienced his perfect love.

Psalm 23:4 (TPT)

Lord, even when your path takes me through the valley of deepest darkness, fear will never conquer me, for you already have! You remain close to me and lead me through it all the way. Your authority is my strength and my peace. The comfort of your love takes away my fear. *I'll never be lonely, for you are near.*

Proverbs 23:26 (NIV)

My son, give me your heart and let your eyes delight in my ways…

Day 33

The Winter Season

Wintertime is an interesting season of life. Everything slows down and, in many places, people stay inside to feel warm and protected from the storms. They are eager for this season to pass because they know that spring will bring the sunshine and all of its warmth, as well as the growth from all the seeds that were planted. The rains will continue to water the soil, and flowers will begin to bloom. I have taken you through a winter season. Even though many of the seeds you have planted have not yet shown much growth, continue to stay faithful and keep yourself close to the warmth of my heart. You are under my protection and I am giving you visions and dreams of what is yet to come in the very next season. You will see new growth and blossoms all around. You are beautiful to me in every season, and when the rain of my Holy Spirit is allowed to touch the soil of your heart, your new growth springs forth, and it is breathtaking. Your aroma is fragrant and sweet.

Scripture Meditation

Song of Songs 2:11-12 (TPT)

The season has changed, the bondage of your barren winter has ended, and the season of hiding is over and gone. The rains have soaked the earth and left it bright with blossoming flowers. The season for singing and pruning the vines has arrived. I hear the cooing of doves in our land, filling the air with songs to awaken you and guide you forth.

Numbers 12:6 (NLT)

And the LORD said to them, "Now listen to what I say: If there were prophets among you, I, the LORD, would reveal myself in visions. I would speak to them in dreams.

2 Corinthians 2:15 (NIV)

For we are to God the pleasing aroma of Christ among those who are being saved and those who are perishing.

Day 34

His Plan for Me

Do not worry about all the details. I want you to step back and look at the bigger picture. Then you will see, with the eyes of your spirit, my revelation of what you are to do. I will take care of the details for you. I am the master of creativity, and I will lead you into unusual circumstances to make known to you what I have been orchestrating for years. Your ways are not my ways. My plans are to prepare you for what is in store for you, and for you to learn how to trust my voice and direction. Leave the details and the other people for me to take care of, and just keep your eyes open so you can see what I am doing all around you. When it is your time to step out, I will lead you. I will gently nudge you when you are uncertain. It is a matter of hearing me, seeing me and trusting me to be there as you step out. I love you, and I will use you in much greater ways than you imagine.

Scripture Meditation

Isaiah 55:8-9 (NKJV)

"For My thoughts *are* not your thoughts, Nor *are* your ways My ways," says the LORD. "For *as* the heavens are higher than the earth, So are My ways higher than your ways, And My thoughts than your thoughts.

Proverbs 3:5-6 (TPT)

Trust in the Lord completely, and do not rely on your own opinions. With all your heart rely on him to guide you, and he will lead you in every decision you make. Become intimate with him in whatever you do, and he will lead you wherever you go. Don't think for a moment that you know it all…

John 14:12 (NLT)

"I tell you the truth, anyone who believes in me will do the same works I have done, and even greater works, because I am going to be with the Father.

Day 35

I Am His Masterpiece

When I am working on you from the inside out, my Spirit permeates your thoughts and your heart. Every part of you is open to my transforming power, so you can walk in obedience to the call I have placed on your life. You will not only walk with wisdom and revelation, but you will walk in power and strength. Never before and never again will there be someone like you. You are truly my masterpiece and it brings me great pleasure to behold what I have created in you—every intricacy and every dot of color. It is indescribably beautiful. Just look and see for yourself how perfect you are as my very own creation. This kind of masterpiece is breath-taking in all its beauty and color. Do not ever be ashamed by what you see in the past, or what you see in the mirror. Just know that I love you, and that each day is different. At the end of the day, when you seek me, I will be right here waiting for you. The more you seek me, the more you will find me. I love you, and I am so proud of who you are and that each day you choose to be with me.

Scripture Meditation

Philippians 2:13 (AMP)

For it is [not your strength, but it is] God who is effectively at work in you, both to will and to work [that is, strengthening, energizing, and creating in you the longing and the ability to fulfill your purpose] for His good pleasure.

Ephesians 2:10 (NLT)

For we are God's masterpiece. He has created us anew in Christ Jesus, so we can do the good things he planned for us long ago.

Deuteronomy 7:9 (NLT)

Understand, therefore, that the LORD your God is indeed God. He is the faithful God who keeps his covenant for a thousand generations and lavishes his unfailing love on those who love him and obey his commands.

Day 36

Free to Live

What I do for you each day is so precious. I need you to trust me that I want only the very best for you. When you humble yourself before me and ask me for what you need, not only will I give you what you need, I will give you abundantly more. I will give you the desires of your heart. I see a heart that is yearning to be healed and whole again. I see a vessel that says, "Yes, Lord!", so I will fill you up to overflowing. I see a child who has found The Father and feels safe again. Take this journey with me and see what I will do. My beauty is all around you to discover and behold. Look at what I am creating just for you. I designed it before you were born, and now I get to watch my plan lived out through your life here on the earth. Oh, what a wonder you are to behold. Now you are free to live and experience all that I have laid out for you. I love you.

Scripture Meditation

Psalm 9:10 (TPT)

May everyone who knows your mercy keep putting their trust in you, for they can count on you for help no matter what. O Lord, you will never, no never, neglect those who come to you.

2 Corinthians 9:8 (TPT)

Yes, God is more than ready to overwhelm you with every form of grace, so that you will have more than enough of everything—every moment and in every way. He will make you overflow with abundance in every good thing you do.

Psalm 139:14 (NIV)

I praise you because I am fearfully and wonderfully made; your works are wonderful, I know that full well.

Day 37

Surrendering My Heart

When you come to me in humility and kneel at my feet, the work I am able to do inside of you is intense. It goes deep and heals areas of your heart that you do not even realize need healing. This simple act of surrender does more to position you to walk out my plan for you, than all your human efforts combined. All you ever need to do is just surrender your heart to me every day. Thank you for giving me this time with you. What I am teaching you in your dreams and in your life circumstances is how to see me and hear me clearly each day. When my plan for you is revealed, you will know it, and you will walk boldly into all that I have for you. You will seize the moment and declare victory for your life and the lives of others. So take all that I'm giving you during our times together, and walk out each day in perfect peace.

Scripture Meditation

Psalm 25:9 (TPT)

Keep showing the humble your path, and lead them into the best decision. Bring revelation-light that trains them in the truth.

Psalm 138:3 (NKJV)

In the day when I cried out, You answered me, *And* made me bold *with* strength in my soul.

1 John 5:4 (NLT)

For every child of God defeats this evil world, and we achieve this victory through our faith.

Day 38

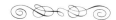

His Keys for Me

Distractions come because the enemy does not want you to see what I am about to show you. You are walking into new territory; new areas in my Spirit. I have keys to give you which will unlock the mysteries of my kingdom power. There is a special table with these keys for you, and you will receive them from me as you enter into my presence each day. I am giving you greater levels of authority. You will fight your battles with greater victory. Your prayers will be more effective than before. Our time together, even when brief, allows you to pick up more of these important keys in your life. Do not get distracted by the things that are pulling your thoughts away from me and my plan for you. Keep focused on me long enough to see what I am telling you to do. You are amazing, and you have been given a unique set of abilities and spiritual gifts. I am watching to see if you will walk through the door and into my presence.

Scripture Meditation

Genesis 13:17 (NKJV)

"Arise, walk in the land through its length and its width, for I give it to you."

Luke 22:29-30 (NLT)

And just as my Father has granted me a Kingdom, I now grant you the right to eat and drink at my table in my Kingdom. And you will sit on thrones, judging the twelve tribes of Israel.

Matthew 16:19 (AMP)

"I will give you the keys (authority) of the kingdom of heaven; and whatever you bind [forbid, declare to be improper and unlawful] on earth will have [already] been bound in heaven, and whatever you loose [permit, declare lawful] on earth will have [already] been loosed in heaven."

Day 39

God's Secrets for My Life

I am doing a new thing in your life right now; something of which you are not yet aware. I have been building something inside of you throughout your whole life, and although there are some things you see clearer than ever before, this new thing is much, much more. I am keeping this secret, even from you. I tell you this now, because I need you to keep your attention on what I am doing in your life. Remember, you are not just living each day simply to be obedient. I have a strategy in place by which I give you more pieces of my plan each day, and the surprise is hidden in the details of these pieces. You can see the scenery, the sky and the general layout of your life's picture, but there are still many more pieces I have hidden from you that have very significant meaning. If you will give me your attention each day, I will give you another piece of my plan. One day you will look at this masterpiece of detail I have put together for you, and the individual pieces will become one brilliant live picture full of color so vibrant you will stand amazed at its beauty. Keep your eyes on me and what I am giving you each day.

Scripture Meditation

Isaiah 43:16-21 (MSG)

This is what GOD says, the God who builds a road right through the ocean, who carves a path through pounding waves, The God who summons horses and chariots and armies—they lie down and then can't get up; they're snuffed out like so many candles: "Forget about what's happened; don't keep going over old history. Be alert, be present. I'm about to do something brand-new. It's bursting out! Don't you see it? There it is! I'm making a road through the desert, rivers in the badlands. Wild animals will say 'Thank you!'—the coyotes and the buzzards—Because I provided water in the desert, rivers through the sun-baked earth, Drinking water for the people I chose, the people I made especially for myself, a people custom-made to praise me.

Daniel 2:22 (AMP)

"It is He who reveals the profound and hidden things; He knows what is in the darkness, And the light dwells with Him.

Matthew 13:35 (NLT)

This fulfilled what God had spoken through the prophet: "I will speak to you in parables. I will explain things hidden since the creation of the world."

Day 40

Am I Listening to Him?

My words are always available to you. You do not have to ask me to speak, because I am always speaking in many different ways. Are you listening? Are you able to set aside the distractions and open up your spiritual ears? I have many things to share with you each day, and my revelation is fresh and new each time you come to me. I want you to seek me first, before the day is filled with other business. What I have to say will affect your day and the decisions you make. Thank you for always trying to listen to me, even in the middle of the day when it is difficult to slow down. Whenever you take a moment to quiet yourself, you will be able to hear me much better. It is my pleasure to set things straight for you and to bring you into your divine appointments that I have already prepared for you. My wisdom will be spoken to others through you, including people with authority over you. They will contemplate the wisdom you share. This is just one more reason that I thank you for taking time in your day to listen to my voice.

Scripture Meditation

Proverbs 1:5 (NIV)

...let the wise listen and add to their learning, and let the discerning get guidance—

Proverbs 3:5-12 (MSG)

Trust GOD from the bottom of your heart; don't try to figure out everything on your own. Listen for GOD's voice in everything you do, everywhere you go; he's the one who will keep you on track. Don't assume that you know it all. Run to GOD! Run from evil! Your body will glow with health, your very bones will vibrate with life! Honor GOD with everything you own; give him the first and the best. Your barns will burst, your wine vats will brim over. But don't, dear friend, resent GOD's discipline; don't sulk under his loving correction. It's the child he loves that GOD corrects; a father's delight is behind all this.

Psalm 62:5 (NLT)

Let all that I am wait quietly before God, for my hope is in him.

Day 41

Endless Revelation

The layers I am revealing to you about my presence and my work in your life are endless. Each day brings new revelation in my Word and through my voice. You never have all of me because there is always more of me to receive, and more of me that you need in order to continue reaching out and giving to others. Without seeking me fresh each day, you will not have the revelation or the strength to accomplish all that I have planned for you. Fan into flames the gift I have placed inside of you. You will see how others around you are touched when you yourself are filled with my power, goodness and peace. You will naturally burn bright and others are drawn to this light. I want you to remember that you have a relationship with all of us: Your Father in Heaven, Jesus and the Holy Spirit. We all love spending time talking with you and helping you experience heaven here on earth. Our love for you is amazing, and it gives us great pleasure to lavish it on you.

Scripture Meditation

Psalm 16:11 (TPT)

For you bring me a continual revelation of resurrection life, the path to the bliss that brings me face-to-face with you.

2 Timothy 1:6 (NLT)

This is why I remind you to fan into flames the spiritual gift God gave you when I laid my hands on you.

Matthew 5:16 (NIV)

In the same way, let your light shine before others, that they may see your good deeds and glorify your Father in heaven.

Day 42

Life to Those Dead Areas

Every day I draw you closer and show you how to walk in my Spirit. Allow me time to change your mindset, because it is so much better for you than walking through the day not thinking about me or even recognizing what I am doing all around you. Taste and see all that I have to give you. Then, after you have been in my presence, I want you to pour out to others my tremendous goodness. I have washed away the mistakes in your past, and I have created for you this beautiful picture of what I have planned for your life. It is a peaceful place—far away from your worries and distractions. The trees, the sun-filled sky and the rivers that surround you are breathtakingly beautiful, and I want you to see in your spirit what I have created for you. Let my river of life flow through you to bring life to those dead areas in your heart. Let me refresh you and restore for you those dreams long forgotten. This is a new day and I will create a new thing for you—just ask me ask to refresh you and fill you with more of my Spirit.

Scripture Meditation

Philippians 2:13 (TPT)

God will continually revitalize you, implanting within you the passion to do what pleases him.

Ezekiel 47:9,12 (NKJV)

And it shall be that every living thing that moves, wherever the rivers go, will live. There will be a very great multitude of fish, because these waters go there; for they will be healed, and everything will live wherever the river goes...Along the bank of the river, on this side and that, will grow all *kinds of* trees used for food; their leaves will not wither, and their fruit will not fail. They will bear fruit every month, because their water flows from the sanctuary. Their fruit will be for food, and their leaves for medicine.

Isaiah 43:19 (NLT)

For I am about to do something new. See, I have already begun! Do you not see it? I will make a pathway through the wilderness. I will create rivers in the dry wasteland.

Day 43

His Unfailing Love

When does my love for you stop? When does my time with you end? Never! The times in your life when you struggle, feel dry and weary or even feel that I have withdrawn from you, are not because my presence has left you. The truth is that my love and presence in your life are constant and never failing. Many times, it is your thoughts and protective emotional walls that have been erected or an unrepentant heart that cause you to feel that I am far away, but I am not. I love you no less than I ever have, and I will never be able to love you more than I already do. My love never fails. No matter what you are going through and no matter how you may feel, I need you to trust me with your pain and your circumstances. Call on me in your distress and I will answer you. I love you, and I am right here with open arms ready to embrace you. Come and discover my unfailing love for you.

Scripture Meditation

Psalm 136:2 (TPT)

Give thanks to God, our King over all gods! His tender love for us continues on forever!

Psalm 86:7 (NIV)

When I am in distress, I call to you, because you answer me.

John 15:9 (TPT)

"I love each of you with the same love that the Father loves me. You must continually let my love nourish your hearts.

Day 44

Receiving His Promises

Do you know what the future holds? Not really, but my promises are "yes and amen", so believe in my Word and receive what I have promised you. You must come into agreement with my Word, by faith, to receive my promises for your life. I offer you so much that you can be absolutely assured of, even though you do not know what tomorrow will bring. That is why I tell you not to worry about tomorrow. Focus on my Word and what I have promised you. Then use the Word, and what it tells you about who I am and who you are, to carry out all that is in front of you. Walk into each day with confidence that I will not let you fall. I will be there to grab your hand and lead you into my peace and rest. I will guide you through your next steps, but only after you have entered into my peace and rest. This way you can hear my instructions clearly. Enter my rest now. Listen to my voice speaking to your heart.

Scripture Meditation

Proverbs 27:1 (NIV)

Do not boast about tomorrow, for you do not know what a day may bring.

2 Corinthians 1:20 (NKJV)

For all the promises of God in Him *are* Yes, and in Him Amen, to the glory of God through us.

Romans 10:17 (NKJV)

So then faith *comes* by hearing, and hearing by the word of God.

Day 45

My Words Create

Not only do my words create change in the world every day, but your words do as well. After you breathe in my Spirit, you are able to breathe out my presence on others. You breathe in my revelation and then speak my words which create change in the world. This is what I have intended for my people to do from the very beginning. Thank you for spending time with me each day trying to discover my plan for you. It has all been written down since before you were born. I am breathing into those pages of your life today, and you will in turn breathe out this wonderful life-giving Spirit of mine on everything you see around you today. You are now prepared to create with your words and your prayers those things I intended for you to create. You are unique and my relationship with you is unique. This is how I work through you and all believers to touch every place and every person on this earth. Thank you for joining me in this beautiful creation today.

Scripture Meditation

Proverbs 18:21 (NIV)

The tongue has the power of life and death, and those who love it will eat its fruit.

Psalm 139:16 (NLT)

You saw me before I was born. Every day of my life was recorded in your book. Every moment was laid out before a single day had passed.

Isaiah 61:1 (NLT)

The Spirit of the Sovereign Lord is upon me, for the Lord has anointed me to bring good news to the poor. He has sent me to comfort the brokenhearted and to proclaim that captives will be released and prisoners will be freed.

Day 46

My Heavenly Father's Correction

Each time you come to me with your tender, open and transparent heart, I wrap my arms around you and tell you that I am right here to love you and comfort you. I do this especially when you are struggling in the flesh, or when you are feeling the pains of my correction. Even though my correction is loving and gentle, you may feel some frustration and disappointment. This is usually because you strongly desire to do the right thing. I see your desire to learn more about my spiritual gifts and how to use them appropriately, so no one gets hurt. That is why it is so important to come to me every day, so I can lovingly prepare you for the great plan I have for your life. Let my love encourage you today, because I am proud of your desire and effort to grow spiritually and take territory for my kingdom. Seek me and grow deeper in my revelation and wisdom. It is all you need to walk safely and powerfully on the earth.

Scripture Meditation

Ezekiel 36:24-26 (NLT)

For I will gather you up from all the nations and bring you home again to your land. "Then I will sprinkle clean water on you, and you will be clean. Your filth will be washed away, and you will no longer worship idols. And I will give you a new heart, and I will put a new spirit in you. I will take out your stony, stubborn heart and give you a tender, responsive heart.

Hebrews 12:5-7 (TPT)

And have you forgotten his encouraging words spoken to you as his children? He said, "My child, don't underestimate the value of the discipline and training of the Lord God, or get depressed when he has to correct you. For the Lord's training of your life is the evidence of his faithful love. And when he draws you to himself, it proves you are his delightful child." Fully embrace God's correction as part of your training, for he is doing what any loving father does for his children. For who has ever heard of a child who never had to be corrected?

Proverbs 2:6 (TPT)

Wisdom is a gift from a generous God, and every word he speaks is full of revelation and becomes a fountain of understanding within you.

Day 47

Am I Too Busy?

Sometimes you do not realize that you are drifting away from the passion in your heart for me and my kingdom work. You may not even feel for a moment that you love me any less, but busyness and weariness can take away our time together—the time you so desperately need. I am glad when you are able to recognize these busy times and surrender yourself to me again. Trust me. As you make time to spend with me each day, you will suddenly feel your strength and your passion increase and my love ignite inside of you. This fresh spark, when fueled with the new wine and fresh breath of my Spirit, will turn into revival fire inside of you. Your focus will turn back to my kingdom plan for your life, instead of it being centered around the list of things you believe need your immediate attention. Come back to me and fan the flame I am igniting inside of you. I love you my child. You are empowered by my Spirit to make such a difference today.

Scripture Meditation

Romans 12:11 (ISV)

Never be lazy in showing such devotion. Be on fire with the Spirit. Serve the Lord.

Ephesians 3:16 (AMP)

May He grant you out of the riches of His glory, to be strengthened *and* spiritually energized with power through His Spirit in your inner self, [indwelling your innermost being and personality]…

Hebrews 13:21 (TPT)

…may he work perfection into every part of you giving you all that you need to fulfill your destiny. And may he express through you all that is excellent and pleasing to him through your life-union with Jesus the Anointed One who is to receive all glory forever! Amen!

Day 48

Let It Rain

When we spend time together and you allow my rain to pour down on you and saturate you with my presence, your eyes are opened and ready to see my glorious work around you. You will see my love for you and what marvelous things I have created for your life. You will see the wonders I plan to do through your life, so never stop letting my Spirit rain on you. Stay saturated with the move of my Spirit, so your eyes may see the glory of my presence and all that I place before you. I prepare the way for you and have given you my promises to lean on every step of the way. Do not lose sight of these promises. They are unbreakable, and as you hold onto them by faith you will see that I am faithful to bring them all to pass. Let the rain keep falling on you and let my rainbow reveal itself to you. I will love you and cherish you for eternity.

Scripture Meditation

Psalm 143:6 (TPT)

Now I'm reaching out to you, thirsting for you like the dry, cracked ground thirsts for rain.

Psalm 16:11 (NKJV)

You will show me the path of life; In Your presence *is* fullness of joy; At Your right hand *are* pleasures forevermore.

Romans 4:20-21 (NIV)

Yet he did not waver through unbelief regarding the promise of God, but was strengthened in his faith and gave glory to God, being fully persuaded that God had power to do what he had promised.

Day 49

Sharing His Goodness with Others

My voice will be heard more clearly today because you have taken the time to tune out the distractions and let go of those things that stood in the way. Come to my banqueting table and feast on the goodness I have prepared for your life. I have so much I want you to experience and enjoy on this earth. All that you need to do is come to me to receive it, so that you can then tell others about what you have tasted. Invite them to come. They need not be hungry or thirsty anymore. Go to the highways and the byways and bid them to come to me. I know that doing this feels uncomfortable at times, but do not become selfish. Do not hold back from helping others receive all that I want them to have. I love you and my Spirit will come upon you with boldness, love and compassion for them. Just trust me and step out by faith as I open the door.

Scripture Meditation

Song of Songs 2:4 (NIV)

Let him lead me to the banquet hall, and let his banner over me be love.

Psalm 34:8 (NASB)

O taste and see that the LORD is good; How blessed is the man who takes refuge in Him!

Matthew 9:36-38 (NLT)

When he saw the crowds, he had compassion on them because they were confused and helpless, like sheep without a shepherd. He said to his disciples, "The harvest is great, but the workers are few. So pray to the Lord who is in charge of the harvest; ask him to send more workers into his fields."

Day 50

The Sacrifice of Praise

I am enlarging your territory right now, and I am enlarging your capacity to receive all that I have for you. Keep coming to me each day and asking me to help you grow. You will need to bring with you the sacrifice of praise, even if you are weary and the storms of life surround you. So come, and do not give in to your flesh, because you are about to receive more favor and abundant provision for your life. I will enlarge your capacity to receive it, and I will enlarge the territory you are gaining for my kingdom. My promised land will be yours to take hold of and subdue. The plunder will be yours, and you will find no end to the riches I will give you in this new land. Come, bring me your weary body and offer me your life as a living sacrifice of praise. I am here waiting to expand your horizons like never before.

Scripture Meditation

Hebrews 13:15 (AMP)

Through Him, therefore, let us at all times offer up to God a sacrifice of praise, which is the fruit of lips that thankfully acknowledge *and* confess *and* glorify His name.

1 Chronicles 4:10 (NKJV)

And Jabez called on the God of Israel saying, "Oh, that You would bless me indeed, and enlarge my territory, that Your hand would be with me, and that You would keep *me* from evil, that I may not cause pain!" So God granted him what he requested.

Exodus 12:36 (NKJV)

And the LORD had given the people favor in the sight of the Egyptians, so that they granted them *what they requested.* Thus they plundered the Egyptians.

Day 51

Loving the Lord with All My Heart

I long to see you worship and receive my love. It is so rare that people can give me all of their heart and attention. I have said in my Word that one of my greatest commandments is to love the Lord your God with all of your heart, with all of your soul, with all of your mind and with all of your strength, but so few are willing to do this. It is not because they do not desire to. It is because they are too busy to even think about it. When you quiet yourself and deliberately rest in my presence, I can fill your heart full of my love and my heart's desire for your life. I can mend those areas of your heart that still need me, and then I awaken your heart to the things I have created you for. Oh, that my people would just come and let me have this time with them. As I love them and heal them, they will see that only through me can this occur. My commandment is not a selfish one, but one of love, so that my people can become all that I have created them to be.

Scripture Meditation

Mark 12:30-31 (NKJV)

"…'And you shall love the LORD your God with all your heart, with all your soul, with all your mind, and with all your strength.' This *is* the first commandment. And the second, like *it, is* this: 'You shall love your neighbor as yourself.' There is no other commandment greater than these."

Luke 10:41-42 (NKJV)

And Jesus answered and said to her, "Martha, Martha, you are worried and troubled about many things. But one thing is needed, and Mary has chosen that good part, which will not be taken away from her."

Psalm 147:3 (AMP)

He heals the brokenhearted And binds up their wounds [healing their pain and comforting their sorrow].

Day 52

My Dreams Are Important

Dreams are powerful, and when you let them speak to you and teach you, they will unravel more of the mysteries of the kingdom. I will use them to heal you and direct you in the way you should go. Pay attention to your dreams. Write them down and ask me to reveal to you their meaning. I will show you things that are very essential for your growth and I will certainly show you the way to find me. It takes time, it takes energy and it takes a desire to go deeper into my revelation for you. When you seek out the deeper things, I will show you even more. I will grab your heart and your thoughts, and I will pull you into an experience with me greater than ever before. It is deep and it is intense sometimes, but your vision and your understanding will grow so much greater when you experience this deeper revelation.

Scripture Meditation

Daniel 7:1 (NIV)

In the first year of Belshazzar king of Babylon, Daniel had a dream, and visions passed through his mind as he was lying in bed. He wrote down the substance of his dream.

Acts 2:17 (NIV)

" 'In the last days, God says, I will pour out my Spirit on all people. Your sons and daughters will prophesy, your young men will see visions, your old men will dream dreams…' "

Psalm 42:7 (NIV)

Deep calls to deep in the roar of your waterfalls; all your waves and breakers have swept over me.

Day 53

His Courtship with Me

Whenever we walk together, my heart is filled with love and joy. Sharing my thoughts with you and hearing yours is the best part of the day. I look forward to our wedding day. I will come for you and we will dance, laugh and experience the most beautiful wedding ever! We will fill ourselves with the best food and the best wine. All of heaven will shout and clap and rejoice in celebration. Even so, this time of courting and romance is a beautiful time as well. Sweetness, tenderness and love surround every day, and everything you do is seen by one whose heart is deeply in-love with you. Cherish these times with me. They are the once-in-a-lifetime moments that you will always remember with great fondness. How you see me, listen to me and talk with me each day lays the foundation of our love for one another. So seek me, watch for me and listen to what I am saying. I want you to know all that you can about me in the Word and through my Spirit. We are one in spirit. My love for you is incredible, and I miss time talking with you when you are too busy. I always look forward to embracing you again soon, and sharing our peaceful, loving moments together. Come and relax with me now and let the breeze of my Spirit blow across your face.

Scripture Meditation

Revelation 19:7 (TPT)

Let us rejoice and exalt him and give him glory, because the wedding celebration of the Lamb has come. And his bride has made herself ready.

Psalm 104:34 (TPT)

May you be pleased with every sweet thought I have about you, for you are the source of my joy and gladness.

I Corinthians 6:17 (NASB)

But the one who joins himself to the Lord is one spirit with Him.

Day 54

My Beautiful Garden

Do you see the hedge of protection I have placed around you? There is plenty of room for you to grow your garden in this area of protection. You can plant trees and vineyards, flowers and every plant that grows beautifully together. The leaves in your garden will not wither. They are abundant and beautiful. You care for your garden and you spend time with me just appreciating everything around you, including your life and your ministry. I have reserved a place right in the middle of this garden where you can come and share with me your thoughts and your plans for future planting. I will never grow weary of hearing all the details of what you enjoy seeing and doing. Thank you for working so diligently; preparing your heart's soil and keeping your garden so beautifully pruned and watered. Your garden is bearing much fruit, and it is a place I enjoy coming to every day. I love you.

Scripture Meditation

Job 1:10 (NKJV)

"Have You not made a hedge around him, around his household, and around all that he has on every side? You have blessed the work of his hands, and his possessions have increased in the land..."

Psalm 1:3 (NKJV)

He shall be like a tree Planted by the rivers of water, That brings forth its fruit in its season, Whose leaf also shall not wither; And whatever he does shall prosper.

Luke 8:15 (NLT)

And the seeds that fell on the good soil represent honest, good-hearted people who hear God's word, cling to it, and patiently produce a huge harvest.

Day 55

His Perfect Peace

Green pastures, breezes blowing through the trees; these are the things one might picture when they think of a peaceful place, but my love for you is perfect peace. When you let my love and my Spirit blow into your life during our times of intimacy together, it leaves you with a heart full of my perfect peace. Breathe me in and let me fill you even more. Experience this feeling of complete rest and peace. You can walk in this always. Even in the midst of the raging waters, my peace around you lifts you above the waters and floats you in a bubble of protection. It is a supernatural grace that comes over you when you just close your eyes and breathe me in. So, continue to do this. Then as you open your eyes, focus on me and feel my peace surround you.

Scripture Meditation

Isaiah 26:3 (NLT)

You will keep in perfect peace all who trust in you, all whose thoughts are fixed on you!

2 Samuel 22:31 (NLT)

"God's way is perfect. All the LORD's promises prove true. He is a shield for all who look to him for protection.

Colossians 3:2 (TPT)

Yes, *feast on all the treasures of the heavenly realm* and fill your thoughts with heavenly realities, and not with the distractions of the natural realm.

Day 56

Tests and Trials

You are indeed getting stronger each and every day. It may seem like you are floundering at times but, in reality, I am just taking you through some necessary tests and trials. The enemy will try and mask these tests as his battle and victory in your life and hopes you will see it as defeat. I am looking at a much bigger picture of the days and seasons in your life when you will need to know for certain who you are in me, and how nothing is too costly for having intimacy with me. Each intimate moment we spend together prepares you for our relationship as bride and bridegroom. I am able to reveal to you another part of me that you have not yet discovered. That is what makes our time together so fun and full of love and passion—discovering our love for one another in a whole new way. You are so precious and beautiful to me. I am here to help you through your tests and trials and teach you more about me and about yourself. You are my heart's desire and I love that I am yours.

Scripture Meditation

1 Peter 1:7 (NLT)

These trials will show that your faith is genuine. It is being tested as fire tests and purifies gold—though your faith is far more precious than mere gold. So when your faith remains strong through many trials, it will bring you much praise and glory and honor on the day when Jesus Christ is revealed to the whole world.

John 3:29 (TPT)

He is the Bridegroom, and the bride belongs to him. I am the friend of the Bridegroom who stands nearby and listens with great joy to the Bridegroom's voice. And because of his words my joy is complete and overflows!

Psalm 54:4 (TPT)

But the Lord God has become my divine helper. He leans into my heart and lays his hands upon me!

Day 57

His Spirit Flows Through
Our Veins

I wish my people would all experience how good it feels to have their hearts fully surrendered to me. It is an experience so amazing, healing and resurrecting. I can take all of their pain, past tragedies and disappointments and transform their lives to be filled with pure joy and passion. Dreams will be resurrected in their hearts and minds again. My love is immeasurable, and it fills every crack and space left void. The love I have heals the broken-hearted and restores their blood flow once again. My Spirit brings life as it flows through their veins and goes right to the heart of the matter. My love is life-changing. It is breathtaking. It is all the world will ever need. Will you tell them for me? Tell them of my love for them. It is so amazing and complete.

Scripture Meditation

Mark 12:30 (NIV)

'...Love the Lord your God with all your heart and with all your soul and with all your mind and with all your strength.'

2 Corinthians 12:9 (TPT)

But he answered me, "My grace is always more than enough for you, and my power finds its full expression through your weakness." So I will celebrate my weaknesses, for when I'm weak I sense more deeply the mighty power of Christ living in me.

1 John 4:10-11 (TPT)

This is love: He loved us *long before we loved him.* It was his love, not ours. He proved it by sending his Son to be the pleasing sacrificial offering to take away our sins. Delightfully loved ones, if he loved us with such tremendous love, then "loving one another" should be our way of life!

Day 58

Leading Others to Jesus

As you grow in your passion to know me and to share my love with others, I will continue to enlarge your capacity to receive my love and power. Out of your life, I will send rivers of living water to those who are thirsting after me. There are people who will in fact die because they cannot break free to find these waters. Set my people free and give them a drink. I need you to keep enlarging your capacity, so you can pour out my living water on a dry and thirsty land. The next generation is longing to see my love and my power. They hear about a man named Jesus, but they have not yet experienced me. They do not understand what it means to be filled with my love, peace, joy and goodness, or what it is to walk in my supernatural power here on the earth. Will you show them for me? Will you come to my fountain of life and drink, so you can show others how to find this life-giving water? I need you to bring them to me.

Scripture Meditation

John 7:38 (AMP)

"He who believes in Me [who adheres to, trusts in, and relies on Me], as the Scripture has said, 'From his innermost being will flow *continually* rivers of living water.' "

Isaiah 44:3 (NIV)

For I will pour water on the thirsty land, and streams on the dry ground; I will pour out my Spirit on your offspring, and my blessing on your descendants.

John 4:14 (NLT)

"…But those who drink the water I give will never be thirsty again. It becomes a fresh, bubbling spring within them, giving them eternal life."

Day 59

Victory!

You have discovered what it means to press in and move forward in my power and strength. You will now be strengthened in your body, soul and spirit because you put your trust in me. There is not one disappointment in life that I will not turn around for my glory, if you will but give it to me to do with as I know best. Trusting me can be one of the most difficult things to learn how to do. It takes a heart for me and the things I am doing above anything else around you. Do not be afraid that you are not strong enough to do it, because with my strength nothing is impossible. You are beyond the point of turning back now. You have already made the decision to press forward to victory, and you have already won. The victory is yours!

Scripture Meditation

1Thessalonians 5:23 (NLT)

Now may the God of peace make you holy in every way, and may your whole spirit and soul and body be kept blameless until our Lord Jesus Christ comes again.

Psalm 28:7 (NIV)

The Lord is my strength and my shield; my heart trusts in him, and he helps me. My heart leaps for joy, and with my song I praise him.

1 Chronicles 29:11 (NLT)

Yours, O Lord, is the greatness, the power, the glory, the victory, and the majesty. Everything in the heavens and on earth is yours, O Lord, and this is your kingdom. We adore you as the one who is over all things.

Day 60

A New Season

I am bringing you into a new season; one where the road will narrow, and your focus will be on the things I have called you to do. I will help you during this time with discipline and patience. I am taking you to a more intensive training ground; one where I will push you and stretch you further than before. You will need to come to my fountain continually and let my drink refresh you. Then I am going to send you back out into the world to do more. Do not be concerned about this season. Be excited, because the obstacles in front of you are about to be moved. Although you will move forward swiftly, you will need to display the fruit of patience that you have developed during this training season. Remember to wait on me, be refreshed by me and receive my Spirit's power. Then, in my perfect time, you will move forward powerfully until we cross the finish line together.

Scripture Meditation

Proverbs 10:5 (TPT)

Know the importance of the season you're in and a wise son you will be. But what a waste when an incompetent son sleeps through his day of opportunity!

Psalm 36:9 (TPT)

To know you is to experience a flowing fountain, drinking in your life, springing up to satisfy. In the light of your holiness we receive the light of revelation.

Psalm 44:5 (TPT)

Through your glorious name and your awesome power we can push through to any victory and defeat every enemy.